This library edition published in 2011 by Walter Foster Publishing, Inc.
Walter Foster Library
Distributed by Black Rabbit Books.
P.O. Box 3263 Mankato, Minnesota 56002

Printed in China, Shanghai Offset Printing Products Limited, Shenzhen.

First Library Edition

Library of Congress Cataloging-in-Publication Data

Wang, Lucy.
    The art of Chinese brush painting / by Lucy Wang. -- 1st library ed.
        p. cm. -- (Artist's library series)
    ISBN 978-1-936309-30-6 (hardcover)
    1. Ink painting, Chinese--Technique. I. Title.
    ND2068.W364 2011
    751.4'251--dc22

                                                                2010005938

032010
0P1815

9 8 7 6 5 4 3 2 1

Artist's Library Series

The Art of
Chinese Brush Painting

by Lucy Wang

Lucy would like to thank Kathleen Wang, whose help in creating this book is greatly appreciated.

Contents

Introduction

People of all cultures are drawn to the simplicity, harmony, and unparalleled grace of Chinese brush painting. Characterized by fluidity and economy of line, this style of art bears a unique appearance that suggests both self-discipline and spontaneity. In line with the Taoist philosophy of the East, the focus of Chinese brush painting is capturing an object's essence and spirit rather than reproducing an object as it is seen. Chinese brush artists therefore use brushstrokes, color, and contrast to reflect and reveal the individual character of a subject.

In this book, you will learn the fundamentals of this elegant art style, including how to hold the brush, how to execute basic strokes, and how to use an ink stick and ink stone. And professional Chinese brush painter Lucy Wang will guide you step by step through a delightful collection of subject matter, from a napping kitten to a traditional Asian landscape. With easy-to-follow instructions, helpful tips, and plenty of inspiration to guide you along the way, this book will provide you with a pleasant and approachable introduction to the art of Chinese brush painting.

History and Philosophy of Chinese Brush Painting

Chinese brush painting is a traditional art form that has been around for more than 2000 years. In the year 200 BCE—during the Han Dynasty—the Chinese began to record their history on sheets of silk, bamboo, and other types of wood. They applied these images using tapered paintbrushes made of wolf hair and soaked in ink made from pine soot and water. Though these first Chinese markings were not accurate representations of what they conveyed, each symbol suggested an object, action, or idea within its strokes. It was from this early form of calligraphy that Chinese brush painting evolved, maintaining the importance of essence over realism. In the year 105 CE, the invention of paper brought new possibilities to the art form, offering a thin, absorbent surface for painting. The availability and convenience of paper also helped Chinese brush painting flourish.

The first account of Chinese brush painting theory surfaced shortly after 500 CE. One of the great masters of the art, Hsieh Ho, formulated six tenets that are still respected and followed today. The basic principles are the following:

1. Enliven the painting with a sense of spirit.

2. Use brushstrokes as a means to suggest character.

3. Understand the natural form of the subject.

4. Apply color that is appropriate for the subject.

5. Create a skillful arrangement of the objects and empty space.

6. Copy and pass on the methods of past masters.

Keep these six principles in mind as you complete the projects in this book. Remember that the aim of Chinese brush painting is to portray an essence, so don't be discouraged if your painting doesn't look completely realistic or lifelike; focus instead on capturing the subject's texture, soul, and energy.

5

Supplies

The art of Chinese brush painting requires four main materials: a Chinese paintbrush, paper, ink, and an ink stone. Called "The Four Treasures" of an artist's studio, these items cover the basics, but there are also several other items that you will need to gather before you begin. When you purchase your supplies, try to buy the best you can afford; better quality products are easier to work with and provide better results than less expensive tools do.

Ink Stick and Ink Stone

The ink for Chinese brush painting comes in the form of a hard stick; it is liquefied with water and ground on the stone. To use an ink stone and ink stick, put about one teaspoon of fresh water in the well of the stone. Then, using a circular motion, quickly grind the ink stick against the bottom of the well of the stone for about three minutes, or until the water becomes thick and dark black. Before each use, make sure your stone is clear of dry ink. Always use fresh water each time you paint, and always grind the same end of the ink stick.

Chinese Paintbrushes

The bamboo brushes used for Chinese brush (sometimes sold under the name "sumi" brushes) are similar to watercolor brushes, but they have bristles that taper to a finer tip. There are two types of bamboo brushes: stiff and soft. The stiff, brown-bristled brushes are more versatile and resilient, making them good for painting leaves and branches. The soft, white-bristled brushes have more flexible bristles, which make them ideal for painting large areas of color and for depicting soft textures, such as animal fur and petals. For best results, use the brushes recommended in each project and that fit the size of your subject. New brushes have sizing in the bristles—a substance that keeps the bristles in their desired shape. Soak your brushes in water to remove the sizing before use.

Papers

You can use many different types of papers for Chinese brush painting. Newsprint is great for practice because it is both absorbent and inexpensive. Watercolor paper is a wonderful painting surface for final artwork because it's versatile and easy to paint on; the paper absorbs the paint just enough without allowing the colors to bleed. Watercolor paper comes in a variety of textures (also called the "tooth"), ranging from coarse to smooth. The three surfaces shown below are the most common. From top to bottom, they are rough, cold-press (medium texture), and hot-press (smooth). As you progress, you may want to try painting on rice paper—the primary painting surface of Chinese brush painters for more than 2000 years. But Chinese brush painting is not limited to paper; you can produce similar fluid effects with surfaces such as wood, pottery, fabric, and silk.

Brush Rest

A brush rest is used to keep the bristles of your brushes protected between uses. Chinese brush rests come in many different styles and are often made of ceramic or metal. Choose whichever type you prefer.

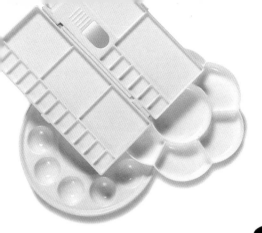

Mixing Palette

Mixing palettes are helpful for diluting your colors and for holding washes for dipping and tipping. (See page 9.) You can also use the sides of the palette wells to help shape the bristles into flattened points. Mixing palettes come in various shapes (round, oval, rectangular, and square) and can be made of a variety of materials (plastic, ceramic, glass, or metal). Plastic palettes are lightweight and reasonably priced, but all types clean up easily with soap and water.

Watercolor Paints

Watercolor paints are often used to add color to Chinese brush paintings. Watercolors are available in several forms and in a range of colors. Tube paints are a popular choice, as they come already moist and ready to use. Just squeeze each color onto a palette well or small dish, and mix it with water to create a wash; the less water there is in the mixture, the more intense the color will be. Pan and cake paints are dry blocks of pigment. To use these paints, add water to loosen the pigment and load your brush with color. Pan colors packaged in a box are convenient, but if you want to mix a lot of color at one time, tube paints are a better choice; you can squeeze out a large amount of pigment quickly and easily.

Water Dish

Chinese brush artists often use small ceramic dishes like the one shown above left to hold clean water for dipping. You should also have an additional jar or bowl for rinsing your brushes between colors. Unless you are double-dipping your colors as directed in a project, always rinse your brush well between colors, and set your brush on a rest when not in use; never let your brushes stand in water.

Other Materials

Aside from the actual painting tools, there are a few extras that will come in handy. Paper towels are great for drying and blotting brushes, as well as for testing colors. You may want to place your paper on felt or use a paperweight to hold it still while you paint to prevent the paper from shifting and curling. To erase any mistakes you make while pencil sketching, use a kneaded eraser rather than a rubber one; kneaded erasers won't damage the surface of the paper, as rubber erasers are prone to do.

Basic Color Palette

Choosing colors can be daunting to beginners, but you don't need to purchase a great array of watercolors to enjoy Chinese brush painting. Just a few basics to add to your black ink will do, and you can always mix just about any other color you may need from these few. Your basic palette of colors should include at least one or two (a warm and a cool version) of each of the primary colors (see page 8), as well as brown and white. As you refine your brush-painting skills and branch out into new subject areas, you will develop your own color preferences. The colors listed below will get you started and are all you need to complete the projects in this book.

- Chinese white
- lemon yellow
- vermilion
- crimson red
- cadmium red
- deep green
- viridian green
- ultramarine blue
- cobalt blue
- indigo blue
- burnt sienna

Color Theory and Mixing

You have already learned that the aim of Chinese brush painting is to convey the essence of a specific subject, and an effective means of capturing this "feeling" on paper is through color. Each color or combination of colors that you select for a subject suggests a particular mood to the viewer; a painting full of reds evokes passion and anger, and a painting made up of soft blues and greens elicits a sense of serenity. Therefore your choice of colors is the key factor in determining whether your painting is a bold, warm piece or a subtle, cool piece. (See "Color Psychology" below.) A basic knowledge of color theory will help you achieve the precise mixes you need for your paintings.

Color Basics

The color wheel provides the perfect starting point for understanding the relationships between colors, which will help you produce the effects you desire. The *primary colors* (red, yellow, and blue) are the three basic colors that can't be created by mixing other colors. All other colors are derived from these three. Each combination of two primaries results in a *secondary color* (purple, orange, or green), and a combination of a primary color and a secondary color results in a *tertiary color* (such as red-orange or red-purple). On the color wheel, at right, the two across from each other are *complementary colors*; they enhance one another when placed together. Groups of adjacent colors are *analogous colors*; when they are used together in a painting, they create an overall feeling of harmony.

Color Wheel

The color wheel is a helpful visual reference that demonstrates color relationships. Knowing the basics of these relationships will help you control the mood and create a sense of unity in your paintings.

Mixing Vivid Secondary Colors

When mixing two primaries to produce a secondary color, you will find that the result varies depending on the hues you choose to mix. Remember that the most vibrant secondary colors are made by mixing two primaries that have the same temperature (i.e., two cools or two warms).

Color Psychology

Colors are often classified figuratively in terms of temperature. The "warm" colors are reds, oranges, and yellows, and the "cool" colors are greens, blues, and purples. But there are variations in temperature within every family of color, or *hue*, as well. A red that contains more yellow, such as cadmium red, is warmer than a red that has more blue, such as alizarin crimson. The temperature of the colors you use can express a mood, season, or the time of day. For example, light pinks, blues, and greens can effectively suggest the fresh air and blooming nature of spring.

Value Scale

Value refers to the relative lightness or darkness of a color or of black. To achieve a range of values with watercolor or ink, simply adjust the amount of water you use in your washes. When creating a wash, it is best to start with the lightest value and build up to a darker wash, rather than adding water to a dark wash.

To get acquainted with the process of creating various values, create a chart like the one above. Apply pure pigment at the left, and gradually add more water for successively lighter values.

Brush Tips

For a flat, dry stroke (near right), dip your brush in color and then press the tip of the brush against the side of a dish or on a paper towel to flatten it and remove excess moisture. Use a flat tip for feathers and flower petals. For a pointed stroke (far right), dip your brush in color and paint with the very tip of the brush. Use a pointed tip for thin lines and details.

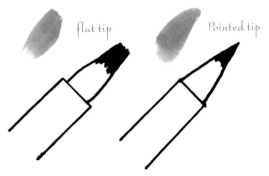

flat tip

Pointed tip

Tipping the Brush

The basic method used in this book for mixing colors on your brush is called "tipping." Start by dipping or fully loading your brush with the first color; then touch the tip of the bristles into the second color. When stroked on the paper, your dipped brush will leave behind an interesting blend of the two colors.

Lemon yellow and ultramarine blue tipped with vermilion

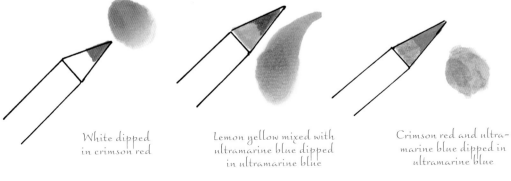

White dipped in crimson red

Lemon yellow mixed with ultramarine blue dipped in ultramarine blue

Crimson red and ultramarine blue dipped in ultramarine blue

9

Handling the Brush

Chinese brush painting is known around the world for its graceful and expressive brushstrokes. To create the fresh and flowing lines, it is important that you hold the brush correctly. Sit up straight and lay the paper on your table or work surface. Place a piece of felt beneath your paper to keep it from sliding and to protect your table. Then practice making the various strokes on these pages using the vertical and slanted holds shown below. These positions may seem awkward at first, but once you get used to them, you will be able to form the strokes correctly.

Slanted Hold

Hold the brush so it's almost parallel to the paper, and use your thumb and fingers to control the movement of the brush, as shown. The width of the stroke is determined by the angle of and the pressure on the brush. The shape of the stroke is determined by movement of the brush: press and lift, push and pull, turn and twist, or dash and sweep.

Vertical Hold

Hold the brush so it's perpendicular to the paper. Grasp the handle just below center, placing it between your thumb and index finger and resting the lower part on the nail of your ring finger. Rest your middle finger on the handle just below your index finger. Support your third finger with your pinkie, and brace the handle with your thumb.

Creating Strokes

Each stroke requires one fluid movement—press down, stroke, and lift. All your brushstrokes should move in a definite direction; you should always be either pushing or pulling your brush. Use your second finger to pull and your third finger to push. Hold the brush gently, letting it lightly touch the paper. Pressing too hard releases too much ink and makes the strokes difficult to control. Practice applying only as much pressure as is needed to create the shape and width of your brushstrokes. It is important to thoroughly practice each stroke and brush position before you begin following the lessons in this book; Chinese brush painting calls for a minimal number of strokes, so each one must be carefully and confidently placed.

Slanted Strokes

Hold the brush almost parallel to the paper and, in one smooth movement, press down, stroke, and lift, using your thumb and fingers to control the movement of the brush. Use slanted strokes to paint large areas and thick shapes.

Vertical Strokes

Hold the brush perpendicular to the paper and stroke from top to bottom, thickening your line by gradually pressing the brush down on the paper. Because this stroke can produce thin lines, it is perfect for outlines, branches, clothing, and other detailed lines.

10

Chinese painting strokes were developed from the strokes of traditional calligraphy (Chinese writing) thousands of years ago. There are three basic strokes derived from calligraphy that you will use throughout this book: the water-drop stroke, which is made by holding the brush in the slanted position, and the bone stroke and the hook stroke, which are both made by holding the brush vertically. Below are a few examples of eight different variations of these strokes for you to follow and practice—remember to keep your wrist and hand loose and flexible as you paint!

Short water-drop stroke: top to bottom

Long water-drop stroke: top to bottom

Reverse water-drop stroke: thicker at top

Water-drop stroke with a thick end

Horizontal bone stroke

Vertical bone stroke

Combined vertical and horizontal bone strokes

Hook stroke: vertical line with a water-drop stroke at the end

Petal and Leaf Strokes

Follow the arrows with your brush to re-create each brushstroke. For thicker lines, press down harder on the brush; for thinner lines, use a lighter touch.

1. Triangle (press down at start, lift for tip)

2. Reverse teardrop (touch tip of brush from top and press down to paper, lifting for tip)

3. Teardrop (press entire brush to paper and lift without moving the brush)

4. Short water-drop

5. Long water-drop

6. Rectangular (even stroke, top to bottom)

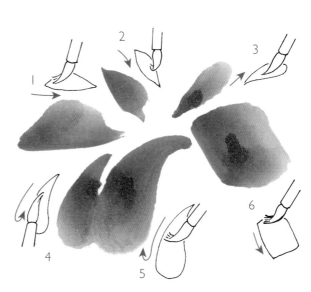

Using Basic Strokes: Bamboo

Bamboo was one of the first subjects to be studied and painted in the Chinese style, so it is fitting that you should begin your practice and preparation with this traditional Chinese plant. Bamboo provides an excellent starting point; the tall, sectioned stalk and long leaves can be easily re-created using the three basic strokes of Chinese brush painting: the bone stroke, the water-drop stroke, and the hook stroke.

Step 1

First saturate a stiff brush with light ink and tip it with dark ink. Then, to paint each section of the stalk, move the brush from the bottom to the top without lifting it off the paper. At the end of each section, stop the brush and lift as you drag slightly to the left to create a bulge or a knot.

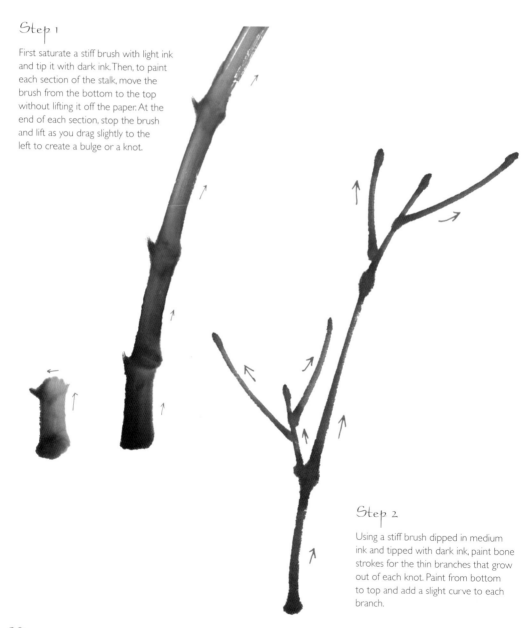

Step 2

Using a stiff brush dipped in medium ink and tipped with dark ink, paint bone strokes for the thin branches that grow out of each knot. Paint from bottom to top and add a slight curve to each branch.

Step 3

Now dip a stiff brush into medium ink and tip it with dark ink. Using long water-drop strokes, hold the brush at a 45° angle and move only the wrist as you paint two long leaves growing from each branch end. Make the leaf clusters fuller by adding a few small leaves.

Step 4

To finish, tip a soft brush with dark ink and paint a thin, curving hook stroke (shown above) across each knot.

Painting flowers

The vibrant colors and soft, curving forms of flowers make them a favorite subject of Chinese brush painters. A great range of brushstrokes and techniques can be used to re-create the various shapes and textures of leaves and petals. Follow the demonstrations below to learn the methods for painting three distinct flowers. As this is the first exercise that involves tipping the brush, notice how the colors interact and blend as you stroke and how the variations in tone create a sense of depth.

Camellia

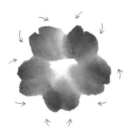

Step 1

Load a large soft brush with a thin white wash and tip it with crimson red. Allow the wash to mix on the brush and then paint two water-drop strokes side by side for each petal, moving from the outer tip of the petal toward the center.

Step 2

Paint five petals in a circular formation to develop the flower, leaving the center unpainted. You may want to rotate the paper as you complete each petal; this way you will not have to change the angle and direction of your strokes.

Step 3

Now load a soft brush with a wash of lemon yellow and deep green and fill in the flower's center. Using a detail brush loaded with thick Chinese white, paint the stamen with thin bone strokes from the tips to the center.

Step 4

Using a very small brush tipped with thick yellow paint, apply dots of pollen in the center of the flower, around the tips of the stamen.

Painting Leaves and Stems

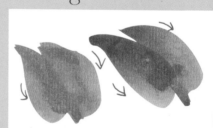

For a blue-green leaf, mix lemon yellow and deep green and load a small stiff brush; then tip it with ultramarine blue and paint two short water-drop strokes. Repeat this process with yellow-green tipped with burnt sienna for a browner leaf, and use less blue for greener leaves. Use a very small brush tipped in a yellow-green wash to paint the stem with bone strokes.

Poinsettia

Step 1
Soak a small stiff brush with a mix of lemon yellow and deep green and tip it with ultramarine blue. Paint a cluster of four round buds, then tip the brush with yellow and add more buds to create an oval shape.

Step 2
Using a soft brush dipped in a vermilion wash and tipped with crimson red, hold the brush at a 65° angle and paint the petals using water-drop strokes. Add a small tip to the middle edge of each petal.

Step 3
Paint the next two petals using the same method as in step two. As you paint each petal, be sure to point the tip of the brush toward the flower's center. Again, it may be easiest to rotate the paper as you paint.

Step 4
Add three more leaves, making each leaf a slightly different length and shape. You may have to apply more than one water-drop stroke for each petal in order to achieve the desired shape.

Step 5
The poinsettia is a full flower, so be sure to fill in any gaps or empty spaces with petals. When you have completed the petals, paint crimson red dots on the green buds with the tip of a small stiff brush.

Bird of Paradise

Step 1
Dip a soft brush in vermilion and tip it with crimson red. Then hold the brush at a 65° angle with the tip facing away from you. Lift up the brush gradually while stroking toward you, controlling the brush's movement with your finger; the angle of the brush will change as it moves.

Step 2
Load a stiff brush with blue, tip it with a small amount of crimson red, and paint water-drop strokes for the petals. Begin with the tip of the brush on the paper and gradually press down at the end. Then hold the brush vertically and add bone strokes for the stem.

Step 3
Mix deep green and lemon yellow with a soft brush and tip it with blue. Allow the washes to blend in the brush and tip it again with crimson red. Holding the brush at a 45° angle, press down from the tip of the sepal and lift the brush up to taper the stroke and finish the sepal.

Step 4
With the same color combination as in the previous step, hold the brush straight up and down and paint the stem with a bone stroke. To create the dry, coarse effect shown at the bottom of the stem, blot the brush on a paper towel before you stroke.

Painting Insects

A common element in Chinese brush paintings, insects usually complement flowers and serve as colorful, intricate focal points. The thin lines and delicate details provide a dynamic contrast to the large, smooth areas of color used to paint flowers. Follow the demonstrations below to practice executing fine details and to gain confidence in using the very tip of the Chinese paintbrush. During this process, remember to keep a fluid simplicity to your brushstrokes and avoid overworking your insects.

Butterfly

Step 1

Use a soft brush with a light ultramarine blue wash tipped with a darker blue wash to paint three water-drop strokes toward the body.

Step 2

Using the tip of a dry stiff brush loaded with black ink, hold the brush vertically and paint the veins of the wings with bone strokes.

Step 3

Holding the brush vertically, paint a dot for the body and bone strokes for the stomach. Create the legs and antennae with bone strokes.

Step 4

To add markings to the butter-fly, dot on small areas of thick white paint. Remember that a butterfly's wings have symmetrical markings.

Dragonfly

Step 1

Saturate a stiff brush with burnt sienna and tip it with crimson red. Paint small water-drop strokes for the eyes and mouth. Using the same color, paint two slanted strokes for the dragonfly's thorax.

Step 2

Using the tip of the brush, paint bone strokes from the thorax to the tip of the abdomen, making the abdomen appear to consist of several segments. The abdomen should be about five times longer than the thorax.

Step 3

Load a soft brush with light ink and tip it with medium ink. Allow the ink to blend within the bristles and then blot the brush on a paper towel. Paint long, rapid water-drop strokes down toward the top of the thorax.

Step 4

Saturate a dry stiff brush with black ink and use the tip to paint thin lines on the dragonfly's wings. Finally tip a clean, dry stiff brush with vermilion and crimson red and paint bone strokes for the legs.

Bees

Step 1

Create a thick yellow wash, load a small soft brush, and tip it with burnt sienna. Paint a small square shape with the tip.

Step 2

Prepare the brush as you did in the previous step, and paint the body of the bee with a fat, rectangular water-drop stroke.

Step 3

Tip the stiff brush with medium ink, blot it on a paper towel, and add the wings with two pairs of thin water-drop strokes.

Step 4

Now add the eyes, antennae, and lines along the wings using a dry stiff brush tipped with dark ink.

Step 5

Finally paint the six legs with black ink using bone strokes and the tip of a detail brush.

Step 1

Dip a small soft brush in thick yellow and tip it with burnt sienna. Using only the tip, paint a small square shape.

Step 2

Load the brush again as you did in the previous step. Then paint the bee's body with one small, fat water-drop stroke.

Step 3

Using a dry stiff brush tipped with medium ink, paint two water-drop strokes on each side of the body for the wings.

Step 4

Use a dry stiff brush and dark ink to paint the eyes, antennae, and lines along the wings. Add stripes on the body.

Step 5

Load a very small, dry brush with black ink, blot it on a paper towel, and use the tip to paint six legs with bone strokes.

fish

Step 1

To paint the body of the fish, load a stiff brush with a vermilion wash and tip it with crimson red. Hold the brush at a 45° angle and swish it in a smooth stroke from the head to the tail, gradually lifting the brush up as you stroke. The curve of the stroke will suggest the movement of the fish's body.

Step 2

With small water-drop strokes, paint two pairs of fins as shown. Then add two water-drop strokes of equal size for the tail, pressing down on the brush at the end of each tail fin.

Step 3

Tip a stiff brush with dark ink and, holding the brush in the vertical position, paint two dots for the eyes. Then paint a dark line down the center of the back as shown.

Painting the Vegetation

Load a small soft brush with thin deep green tipped in crimson red. Then, holding the brush horizontally, apply dots of varying size to suggest the vegetation on the water. Next mix a cooler green by adding a touch of blue to the thin green wash, and randomly apply some more dots, slightly varying the size and shape, as shown in the example. Don't add too much vegetation; you just want to create the essence of the plants to add interest to your composition.

Step 4

To make the black fish, follow the same procedure using medium ink tipped with dark ink for the body.

Step 5

Now use your knowledge of painting fish to create a final composition. Fish should be painted in odd numbers or in pairs, and all the fish should swim in the same general direction. Add a few dots sparingly between the fish to suggest vegetation (see the box on page 18), being careful to preserve the simplicity of the painting.

Cocker Spaniel

Step 1

First lightly sketch the shape of the dog with a pencil. Then use a dry stiff brush tipped with black ink to paint a small dot for the dog's eye and a triangle pointed downward for the nose. Wash out the brush and saturate it with medium ink. Wipe the brush on a paper towel to dry it slightly, and then use the tip to outline the shape of the dog's head, holding the brush vertically.

Step 2

Use medium ink to complete the outline of the dog's body. Keep in mind that cocker spaniels have long hair on their legs, making them look wider than they really are. To show the hair on the feet, behind the leg, and on the belly, apply a few short strokes, rather than making a smooth, continuous line.

Step 3

With a soft brush loaded with medium ink and dipped halfway into dark ink, paint a curved water-drop stroke. Start by placing the tip of the brush at the top of the dog's ear, gradually pressing down more on the brush as your hand turns, following the shape of the ear. Finally paint a short black line with the tip of your brush for the tail.

Step 4

Soak a soft brush with medium ink and tip it with dark ink. Dry the brush slightly on a paper towel and paint the dog's coat markings using three connecting water-drop strokes for each pattern.

Panda

Step 1

Begin by using a pencil to lightly sketch the shape of the panda's head, body, and limbs. Then saturate the soft brush with dark black ink and paint oval-shaped eye patches that slant at a 45° angle. Add a triangular nose and two C-shaped ears, leaving a white space in the center for the opening of the ears.

Step 2

Next load the dry stiff brush with medium-dark ink and use it to paint a thin outline of the panda's face and body. Make sure that the wash is noticeably lighter than the dark ink used for the eye patches and ears; this will ensure that the outline doesn't stand out too much compared to the panda's markings.

Painting the Bamboo

Soak the very tip of the stiff brush with a light green wash and then tip it with dark green. Then use the very tip of the brush to paint thin bone strokes for the branches. Next, to form the leaves, begin with a point on the branch, press down on the brush, and quickly lift up. When making your strokes, follow the directions of the arrows in the example.

Step 3

Next paint the front and back legs on the panda's left side using the soft brush. Saturate the brush with medium ink and dip it in dark black ink; then press down firmly. Soak the brush with dark ink and dip the tip into a small amount of water; then dry the brush on a towel to create a medium-dark ink. Now paint the two legs on the panda's right, starting from the top and moving the brush down to the end of the foot. Be sure to leave a small white gap between each leg to keep them from blending into one another.

Step 4

Now add the bamboo stalk, starting with the branch. Each branch should hold only two large and two small leaves. You may want to add another layer of black ink to the darkest areas of the panda; this will create a stronger contrast against the white.

Kitten

Step 1

Begin by outlining the kitten with pencil. Then dip a stiff brush into a dark wash of dark ink and blot the brush on a paper towel before tracing over the sketch of the kitten's ears, eyes, nose, and mouth with long, fluid bone strokes. Next wash out your brush and mix some medium-light ink. Outline the head with bone strokes and paint several light dots on the kitten's mouth to suggest the base of the whiskers.

Step 2

Now use light ink to outline the body with bone strokes, beginning with the shoulder. Trace over the rest of your pencil marks with a dark gray ink wash, making sure that the brush is not overloaded with ink. Then saturate a soft brush with light ink and dip it in dark ink. Dry the brush and hold it at a 45° angle to paint the tip of the tail with one quick stroke.

24

Step 3

Saturate a small soft brush with a light wash of black ink and tip it with dark ink. Dry the brush on a paper towel and hold it at a 45° angle to paint black stripes on the head, body, and tail. Begin painting these stripes at the edge of the back, curving down to the right to suggest the rounded upper body. Do the same for the hind leg, beginning the strokes at the left and curving them over and down.

Step 4

Next saturate a small soft brush with a medium wash of black ink and stroke light gray over the black marks. (Be careful not to paint over areas that should remain white, such as the ears, face, and lower leg.) Now create the kitten's whiskers using a stiff brush. Load it with very black ink and blot it well on a towel, forming the tip to a dry and straight point. Then hold the brush upright and stroke outward from the little dots on the sides of the mouth. Paint rapid bone strokes with the tip of the brush and keep them simple, with only three whiskers on each side. For the pink areas, load a soft brush with a thin wash of crimson red and blot away excess moisture. Then paint a small pink dot on the nose, line the lower lid of each eye, and add a little pink in the center of both ears.

frog

Step 1

First lightly draw the shape of the frog with a pencil. Then use a stiff brush tipped with dark ink to paint two water-drop strokes for the circular eye, leaving a small white highlight at the top, between the two strokes. After allowing the ink to dry, saturate the soft brush with a vermilion wash and tip it with crimson red. Blot the brush on a paper towel; then paint the top of the head using water-drop strokes, surrounding the eye with color.

Step 2

Using a soft brush dipped in a vermilion wash and tipped with crimson red, paint a long water-drop stroke from the neck to the frog's rear. Then add a series of water-drop strokes along the frog's back, sweeping downward and over the foreleg. Next saturate the soft brush with light ink tipped with a vermilion wash and paint a water-drop stroke from the chin down to the top of the chest, leaving a white spot at the corner of the frog's mouth.

Painting the Front Leg

Using a stiff brush dipped in light ink and tipped with dark ink, paint the remainder of the forelegs with water-drop strokes. Add the toes using small bone strokes, pressing down the brush tip at each joint. To paint the legs farthest from the viewer, use light ink.

Painting the Back Leg

Dip the stiff brush in light ink, tip it with dark ink, and paint the hind leg with two overlapping water-drop strokes. Reload the brush and blot the excess wash on a paper towel. Holding the brush vertically, paint the toes with bone strokes.

Step 3

Paint the legs and feet following the instructions in the box on page 26. Then tip a dry soft brush with light ink and fill in the empty space on the frog's chest. Rinse the brush and load it with a light wash of deep green for the frog's underside. After rinsing the brush again, load it with light ink and outline the belly of the frog. Paint two dots on the frog's backside and add spots to the forearm. Then dry the brush, tip it with dark ink, and paint a dot for the nostril. Add a thin line to define the mouth and another thin line that extends from the corner of the eye outward.

Step 4

Now create a background for the frog by placing him on an anthurium leaf. First add the *spadix*—the curved spike at the flower's center. Saturate a stiff brush with a medium crimson red wash and tip it with a darker, thicker crimson red wash; then apply a long water-drop stroke from the top curving down to the center of the leaf. Use the point of a clean stiff brush tipped with a thick wash of lemon yellow to add equally spaced dots to the crimson spadix. Next tip a dry stiff brush with medium ink and outline the main leaf with long, gently curving strokes. Then rinse out the brush, load it with a wash of lemon yellow and deep green, and highlight areas of the outlines. Tip the same brush with a crimson red wash and add one thick stroke for the stem.

Rabbit

Step 1

Load a soft brush with medium black ink and tip it with dark black ink to paint a water-drop stroke from the nose to the back of the head.

Step 2

Then paint a water-drop stroke beginning at the left point of the first stroke and sweeping under the eye. Add a triangular nose with a brief, downward stroke.

Step 3

Use a soft brush dipped in medium ink and tipped with dark ink to paint the rabbit's ears, using long water-drop strokes. Then add a thinner stroke that connects the tip to the base of the rabbit's right ear, leaving a slender space of white that suggests a fold.

Step 4

Use a dry stiff brush tipped in dark ink to add the eye, leaving a space between the eyeball and the eye socket. Finally paint the mouth, cheeks, and whiskers with bone strokes using medium ink.

Painting the flowers

Load a soft brush with a wash of lemon yellow and deep green tipped with a pure lemon yellow wash. Hold the brush with the handle nearly parallel to the paper, press down, and lift to create the stamens of the flowers.

Dip the brush into a light wash of white, tip it with ultramarine blue wash, and then tip it again with a small amount of crimson red wash. Flatten the brush tip and paint the petals from the outer tips to the edge of the stamen.

Load the brush with a wash of lemon yellow mixed with green deep; then tip it with a wash of ultramarine blue. Use thick, fat water-drop strokes to paint leaf clusters. Vary the size and shape of each leaf to add interest.

Dip the brush into a wash of lemon yellow and tip it with a crimson red wash. Use a series of thin bone strokes to create the stems. Alter the direction of the brush after each bone stroke to give the appearance of knots at the joints.

Step 5

Dip a soft brush in medium ink and blot it on a paper towel. Then outline the rabbit's body using curved bone strokes. Begin each stroke with pressure on the brush tip, and then lift up slightly as you pull the brush along. As each stroke comes to a finish, apply more pressure again at the tip.

Step 6

Load a soft brush with medium ink and tip it with dark ink. Create the rabbit's black markings with large water-drop strokes, beginning at the back and sweeping down.

Step 7

Finally add color and balance your painting with a few blue flowers, following the steps shown in the box on page 28.

Lotus flower and Bees

Step 1

First sketch the lotus flower and bees in pencil. Then load a large stiff brush with a wash of lemon yellow and deep green, tip the brush with ultramarine blue, and paint a dot in the middle of the leaf. Next paint the leaf in three equal sections, using three long water-drop strokes for each section. Paint outward from the center dot, leaving a small white space between the dot and the leaf.

Step 2

To finish the leaf, tip the brush in a yellow or burnt sienna wash (to add variety to the green) and fill in the areas between the three sections of the leaf.

Step 3

Now saturate a large soft brush with a thin white wash and tip it with crimson red. Then apply the front layer of the flower petals with water-drop strokes, following the directions of the arrows.

Step 4

Tip the brush again in the crimson red wash and outline the petals that are farthest from the viewer. Now load a soft brush with a yellow-green wash and fill in the seedpod inside the flower.

Step 5

Still using crimson red, add the two flower buds; then tip some yellow-green on the tip of the bud on the left to indicate the seedpod. Next use a large stiff brush soaked in a yellow-green wash and tipped with ultramarine blue to paint some of the stems with long bone strokes. Paint the remainder of the stems in the same manner using a stiff brush loaded with yellow-green and tipped with crimson red. Then paint the profile of a leaf above the flowers. Add a leaf bud below the large central leaf.

Step 6

Use a stiff brush tipped with deep green to paint dots along the stems. Next outline the seedpod with a very small brush dipped in dark ink. After rinsing out the brush, tip it with lemon yellow and paint small, fat water-drop dots for the stamens around the seedpod. Finally paint the bees by following the chart on page 17.

Horse

Step 1

First sketch the horse's body in pencil. Then load a soft brush with a thinned mix of burnt sienna and medium ink, dip the tip into a pure burnt sienna wash, and paint a diamond-shaped outline for the star on the horse's forehead. Tip the brush with burnt sienna again and paint the nose with two water-drop strokes. Add another small water-drop stroke for the chin.

Step 2

Now dip the tip of the brush in a burnt sienna wash and paint a long water-drop stroke with a crisp, curved edge to create the cheek. Connect the nose and chin with a short stroke.

Step 3

Next tip the brush with black ink and paint two water-drop strokes for the ears. Tip the brush with dark black ink, blot the brush on a paper towel, and paint the nostril and the eye.

Step 4

Rinse the brush well and saturate it with a mix of thinned burnt sienna and medium ink. Apply two long water-drop strokes from the top of the head to the bottom of the neck, using small strokes where needed to connect the neck and head.

Step 5

Load the brush with a wash of burnt sienna and medium ink and tip it with a thicker wash of burnt sienna. Holding the brush at a 65° angle, paint from the top of the back to the bottom of the horse's sides with slightly curved strokes. Leave the stomach white.

Step 6

Now mix light ink with a wash of burnt sienna and tip the brush with black ink. Paint two water-drop strokes to create the chest. Next tip the brush with a pure burnt sienna wash and paint the horse's front left leg from the shoulder to the knee with bone strokes, turning the brush to create the lower section of the leg. When you paint the horse's knees, press down on the brush tip a bit harder to create a knotlike form. Then use the same brush to outline the horse's hoof. Paint the other legs the same way, but use a lighter wash for the two legs farthest away to suggest distance. Next add a thin stroke under the stomach.

Step 7

Load a stiff brush with dark ink. Flatten the tip of the brush by stroking the brush along the rim of a dish or palette well. For the mane, paint strokes from the top of the neck outward, lifting the brush as you stroke to taper the ends of the hair. Next mix light ink with a small amount of burnt sienna and load the brush. Tip the brush with dark ink and paint several curved water-drop strokes, starting with the tip of the brush at the horse's rear and gradually pressing down as you stroke. At the end of each stroke, quickly lift up the brush. When you paint the background, you'll want to cover the top half of the horse with a paper towel so that you don't accidentally splash it with color. Soak the brush with a wash of deep green and hold the brush a few inches from the paper in a horizontal position. Tap the end of the brush handle with your index finger so that tiny droplets of paint spatter over the paper. Then repeat this same process using a wash of crimson red and ultramarine blue (a blue-violet color). When the colors are dry, paint horizontal strokes of a lighter wash of deep green for the ground.

Penguins

Step 1

First determine the position and form of each penguin by creating a light sketch in pencil. Make sure that each penguin is slightly different from the others so the composition isn't too symmetrical.

Step 2

Then paint the head of one penguin with a soft brush dipped in medium ink and tipped with dark ink. Start with a water-drop stroke from the forehead to the back of the head. Holding the brush vertically, paint the beak with the point of the brush and follow with a water-drop stroke down through the throat.

Step 3

Now, still using the soft brush that has been dipped in medium ink and tipped with dark ink, apply a water-drop stroke from the base of the penguin's head over the shoulder and down the side of the body. With the same brush dipped in dark ink and held vertically, sweep from the shoulders to the tips of the wings.

Step 4

Next load a stiff brush with light ink, tip it with medium ink, and paint the outline of the body, legs, and tail with quick, brisk strokes.

Step 5

Repeat steps 2–4 for the other two penguins.

Step 6

Using a soft brush tipped in a vermilion wash, apply short strokes for the bottom of the legs and webbed feet. To paint the glacier, dip a stiff brush in medium ink, tip it with medium-dark ink, and wipe the brush on a paper towel until it is only moist. Holding the brush at a 30° angle and beginning at the peaks, paint the outline of the mountains with downward strokes. Then use a soft brush dipped in a very light wash of ultramarine blue to stroke in icy blue shadows in the snow.

Calico Cat

Step 1

First sketch the outline of the cat. Then saturate a small stiff brush with a lemon yellow wash, blot it on a paper towel, and paint a dot for the eye with a small, rounded water-drop stroke. Using a soft brush tipped in dark ink, outline the eye with the brush point and add dots for the base of the whiskers. Tip the brush with medium ink and finish the outline of the cat's face and body with a series of bone strokes.

Step 2

Saturate a soft brush with light ink tipped with dark ink and dry the brush slightly on a paper towel. Apply a water-drop stroke from the top of the head around the ears, leaving the ears unpainted. Continue to add markings along the top of the cat's back with water-drop strokes. Using the same brush dipped in light ink and tipped in dark ink, start at the tip of the tail and stroke in a curved line to meet the cat's rear marking. For the whiskers, use a dry stiff brush moistened with dark ink to paint several thin bone strokes from the side of the cat's mouth outward. Then add the dark spot for the nose and the short line indicating the mouth. Finally, using the same brush, paint a thin vertical line to indicate the cat's pupil.

Step 3

Rinse the soft brush and load it with a light wash of burnt sienna tipped with darker burnt sienna. With water-drop strokes, paint reddish-brown markings on the cat's ears, face, and back.

38

Painting the flowers and the Butterfly

To create the blossom, dip a soft brush in a light crimson red wash, tip it with a darker crimson red, and paint five rounded water-drop strokes for the petals. For the flower's stamen, saturate a stiff brush with dark ink and blot it on a paper towel. Use only the tip of the brush to paint a small circle in the center and several lines radiating out.

To paint the sepal—which can be seen only on buds and flower profiles—use dark ink to add a short stem and two small water-drop strokes at the base of the flower. The water-drop strokes should curve slightly and rest perpendicular to the stem. Use only three petals to show flowers from a side view. For each bud, simply paint one dot.

For the butterfly, soak a stiff brush in a wash of lemon yellow, tip it with burnt sienna, and paint four water-drop strokes as shown, making the top two sections of the wings longer than the bottom sections. For the butterfly's body, tip a stiff brush in dark ink and indicate the antennae, body, legs, and black markings on the wings.

Step 4

Now add a colorful plum branch and butterfly (demonstrated in the box above) to complement this adorable cat. For the branches, load a stiff brush with light ink and tip it with dark ink. Holding the brush vertically, paint the branches with bone strokes.

Tiger

Step 1

First lightly sketch the tiger with a pencil. Copy what you see, being careful to imitate the angle of the head, the folds in the skin, and the stripes on the face.

Step 2

Now use the fine point of a dry soft brush and medium-dark ink to outline the entire tiger. Start with the eyes, and then paint the nose, mouth, ears, and body. Use more pressure for thick lines and lift the brush to taper the stroke for thin lines.

Step 3

Use the same brush and dip it in medium-dark ink to paint stripes that curve down from the top of the back to the side of the body. Keep in mind that the markings do not necessarily connect from top to bottom; the stripes appear more realistic when broken up. For the tail, paint curved black stripes that continue to the solid, dark tip.

40

Step 4

Next mix a light yellow wash with small amounts of burnt sienna and light black or ink. Use a soft brush to layer this color on the tiger's head and body. Begin from the top of the back and continue down the side of the body, but leave the stomach and the area around the eyes white. When the color dries, stroke burnt sienna over the face and the black stripes. The forehead, nose, cheeks, and top of the back should all be darker. (If the color bleeds into areas that are meant to be white, use white paint to cover the color.) Mix a thin wash of lemon yellow to fill in the eyes.

Step 5

With a dry stiff brush saturated with dark ink, retrace the outline of the face and some of the stripes on the body to make them more distinct and to create variations in the stripes' values. It is not necessary to highlight every stripe; make the markings most intense on the back and keep the markings on the stomach medium gray. For the whiskers, use a dry stiff brush with black ink and begin painting from the black markings above the mouth. Be sure to use rapid strokes to create thin dry lines. To finish, dip the tip of a dry brush into dark ink to paint the pupils of the eyes. Then use thick white paint to add a light reflection in the upper edge of the pupils.

Monkey

Step 1

First draw the outline of the monkey in pencil. Mix a wash of ultramarine blue and paint a horizontal stroke across the monkey's forehead with a stiff brush; then trace around the heart-shaped nose (A). Next rinse out the brush and paint the eyes, ear, and outline of the nose with dark black ink (B).

A

B

Step 2

Now load a soft brush with a wash of burnt sienna and light ink and tip it in black ink; brush on a semi-circle for the head and two water-drop strokes for the shoulders. Tip the brush again with dark ink and paint a horizontal line across the forehead for the hairline. Then load a stiff brush with a light wash of burnt sienna and black ink, blot the brush well on a paper towel, and add small swipes of the brush along the monkey's face to suggest wisps of hair.

Step 3

Load a soft brush with a wash of burnt sienna and tip it with dark ink for the monkey's coat. Begin your first stroke at the lowest point of the back—between the shoulders—and sweep up and around the monkey's rear, keeping the darker tip of the brush along the pencil outline. Then paint several strokes from the monkey's back across and down the side of the body, lifting the brush after each stroke to create a coarse trail. Now dip the brush into the burnt sienna wash and tip it in a thicker wash of burnt sienna to add multiple shades of brown to the brush. Paint the tail in one long, continuous stroke from the tip of the tail to the monkey's rear.

Painting Peaches

Using a thin mix of yellow and green tipped with crimson red, paint two water-drop strokes beside one another to make each peach. Then use a mix of yellow and green tipped with blue to create the leaves with small water-drop strokes.

Painting a Tree Branch

For the branch, load a stiff brush with medium-light ink and paint the outline of the branch. Fill in the branch with several light strokes, reserving the lightest strokes for the center.

Step 4

Saturate a soft brush with burnt sienna mixed with light ink. Tip the brush in dark ink and paint water-drop strokes from the shoulder to the hand. Then use the tip of the brush to paint a thin, curved line along the outline of the stomach.

Step 5

Use the same wash from step three to paint the monkey's legs, starting from the top and lifting the brush slightly as you taper down to the feet. Then tip the brush with a darker wash of burnt sienna mixed with dark ink and paint the individual toes and fingers with thin, controlled strokes. Add colorful background elements, following the instructions in the box above.

Elephant

Step 1

After lightly outlining the elephant in pencil, load a soft brush with a thin mix of burnt sienna and a bit of black ink. Tip it with medium-dark ink and, holding the brush vertically, make a fluid, sweeping stroke from the tip of the trunk to the forehead.

Step 2

Now paint a large water-drop stroke from the elephant's mouth to the chin, finishing the head.

Step 3

Next tip the brush with medium-dark ink and paint a heart shape for the right ear, holding the brush at a 45° angle. Tip the brush with a wash of burnt sienna and paint the left ear with one stroke, leaving a small white space between the ears and the head.

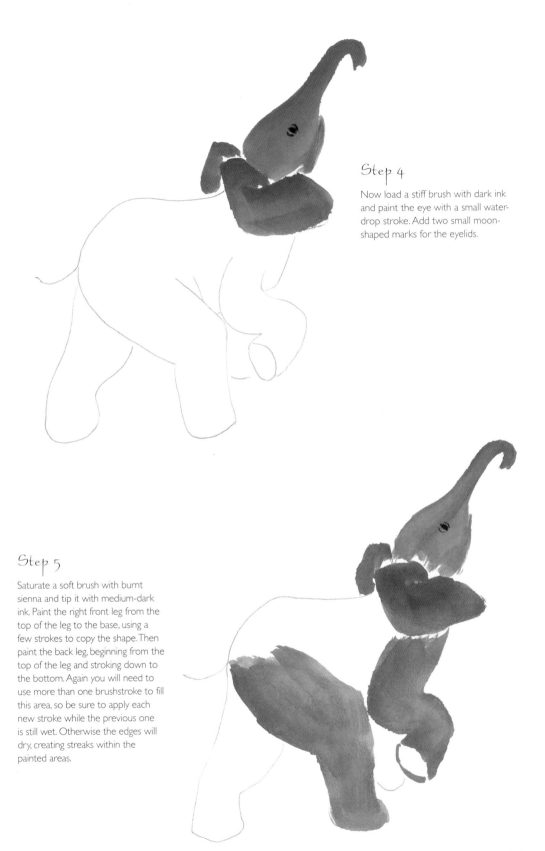

Step 4

Now load a stiff brush with dark ink and paint the eye with a small water-drop stroke. Add two small moon-shaped marks for the eyelids.

Step 5

Saturate a soft brush with burnt sienna and tip it with medium-dark ink. Paint the right front leg from the top of the leg to the base, using a few strokes to copy the shape. Then paint the back leg, beginning from the top of the leg and stroking down to the bottom. Again you will need to use more than one brushstroke to fill this area, so be sure to apply each new stroke while the previous one is still wet. Otherwise the edges will dry, creating streaks within the painted areas.

Step 6

Using a soft brush saturated with burnt sienna and tipped with medium-dark ink, paint several large water-drop strokes, swooping from the neck and curving over the elephant's backside. Add one stroke from the elephant's back curving down to the underside, but be sure to leave a gap of white between the legs and the stomach. Then use a dry stiff brush tipped with dark black ink to paint the tail with a long, thin, continuous stroke.

Painting the Trees

Saturate a dry stiff brush with a medium value of black ink and tip it with a dark value of black ink. Then paint the tree trunk and branches using bone strokes. To create the illusion of a round trunk with dimension, use a lighter value of ink in the center of the brush and a darker value in the outer bristles.

For the green leaves, load a small stiff brush with a mixture of lemon yellow and deep green, and then tip it with ultramarine blue. Next flatten the brush tip on the side of a dish or mixing palette. Hold the brush at an 80° angle, and paint small clusters of leaves by dotting the brush on the paper. Overlap the dots to create depth and texture. Paint the red leaves the same way you painted the green leaves, but use vermilion tipped with crimson red.

Step 7

Using a soft brush dipped in thinned burnt sienna and a small amount of light ink, stroke from the top of the elephant's left leg to the bottom of the foot with a slight water-drop motion. Then paint the right front leg with one small water-drop stroke. For the elephant's toenails, tip the brush with medium-dark ink and paint a few dots along the bottoms of the feet. Load the tip of a stiff brush with a very light wash of thinned ultramarine blue and paint small droplets of water, starting at the tip of the trunk. For the mountain, load a soft brush with a light ultramarine blue wash and tip it with medium blue. Place the brush bristles onto the paper so that the tip is away from you and the bristles are lying flat against the paper. The handle should be leaning toward your face. Then pull the brush to the left and slightly toward you while slowly lifting the brush back to the vertical position. Using a stiff brush loaded with a wash of burnt sienna and black ink, paint thin bone strokes for the surface of the ground. Then use a mix of lemon yellow and deep green tipped with pure deep green to fill in the area below this line. Finally add the trees and flowers as shown in the box on page 46.

Iris and Hummingbird

Step 1

After sketching the whole scene in pencil, prepare a violet wash using a mix of cobalt blue and crimson red. Load a soft brush with the mixture and then dip it in pure water, creating a medium violet wash within the brush. Tip the brush with the initial violet wash, hold the brush at a 65° angle, and paint the first petal from top to bottom with a long, curved water-drop stroke. To modify the size and shape of the petal, add water-drop strokes to either side of the initial stroke.

Step 2

Using the same strokes that were used in step 1 and following the arrows in the example, paint a second petal to the right of the first. For the third petal (at the top), tip the brush with a bit of water before applying the color. (Remember that each petal grows from the center point.) For the fourth petal (at the bottom), use a series of water-drop strokes to create the shape, gradually making each stroke shorter.

Step 3

Tip the brush with cobalt blue to paint the fifth petal (on the left). Then tip the brush with violet to alter the color for the sixth petal (on the right). This variation in color within the flower will give the blossom a sense of depth and keep it from appearing flat on the paper.

Step 4

Mix a lemon yellow and deep green wash with a large stiff brush and tip it with crimson red. Paint the sepals from the base of the flower outward with water-drop strokes; then paint the stems with long, thin bone strokes. Load a soft brush with a violet wash to add a round bud, placing a bit of lemon yellow wash in the center of the flower petals for the stamen.

49

Step 5

Tip a stiff brush in dark ink and blot it on a paper towel. Then hold the brush at a 65° angle and paint a water-drop stroke from the tip of the bird's beak toward the face, adding more pressure to the brush at the end of the stroke. Use the same brush to paint two small dots for the eye, leaving a white space for the highlight. Finally paint the wispy black feathers around the eye with short, quick strokes.

Step 6

Load a small soft brush with a blue-green wash of viridian green and cobalt blue. Tip the brush with a pure cobalt blue wash and paint the top of the head with a water-drop stroke, starting from the beak. Add two smaller water-drop strokes to form the back of the neck. Then paint several water-drop strokes for the base of the wings, dipping again in the light blue-green and tipping in cobalt blue.

Step 7

Now load a stiff brush with medium ink and flatten the tip by running the brush along the edge of a dish or palette well. Starting from the end of the beak, paint outward strokes to create a triangular throat. Use the same brush to outline the stomach. Then dip a stiff brush into medium ink and tip it with dark ink to paint feathers on the wings using long water-drop strokes, pressing down at the end of each stroke.

Step 8

Next load a soft brush with a light blue-green wash and paint water-drop strokes within the tail. Then, without rinsing the brush, tip the brush in light ink and fill in the layer beneath the tail with gray strokes. Now tip a stiff brush in dark ink and paint the bird's feet with small bone strokes.

Step 9

Mix a thick wash of white paint and use a stiff brush to paint rows of dots on the bird's head. Then apply a thin layer of cobalt blue on the top of the head. Now use a soft brush tipped with burnt sienna to add a light brown to the bird's underside.

To create the leaves, mix a wash of lemon yellow and deep green with a large stiff brush and tip it with ultramarine blue. Paint each leaf from top to bottom, lifting the brush as you stroke down. Then tip the brush with a crimson red wash and add the leaf in the background.

female figure

Step 1

Begin by sketching the outline of the figure on paper. Next use a very small brush dipped in medium ink to retrace the image with long bone strokes, blotting the brush on a paper towel to create a coarse, controlled line. (If you wish to trace the exact figure from this project, you can make an enlarged photocopy of step one and place rice paper on top for tracing.)

Painting the Head

Create a light vermilion wash to produce a pale peach color. Saturate a small soft brush with the peach wash, and fill in the woman's face and neck. Leave the nose unpainted to suggest a highlight.

After the face dries completely, load the same brush with a light crimson red wash and blot it on a paper towel to dry it slightly. Then stroke the brush lightly over the upper cheeks, giving the woman a blushed appearance.

Next paint the eyes with a very small, dry brush and thick, dark ink. Then, using thick white paint and the tip of a brush, dot highlights on each eye. Paint the hair with short strokes of dark ink and the flattened tip of a small soft brush.

Step 2

Paint the head as demonstrated in the box on page 52; then fill in the hands with the same light vermilion wash used on the face. Load a large soft brush with a cadmium red wash and apply color generously within the outline of the robe. Then, using a small soft brush, paint the edge of the robe with black ink and paint the ribbon with a cobalt blue wash.

Step 3

Next go over the outline of the robe again with a very small brush dipped in dark crimson red. Apply a wash of light burnt sienna over the folds of the skirt with a soft brush. To create the skirt cover, use a soft brush dipped in a dark wash of cobalt blue. Now paint on the woman's bracelet with a light blue-green wash and a very small brush; then add the hair ornaments using cobalt blue, light blue-green, and cadmium red.

Step 4

Fill in the fan using a small soft brush dipped in light ink. After the ink dries, tip the brush in dark ink to create the frame of the fan and to paint the small bamboo design. Next add the cluster of bamboo leaves above the figure using the tip of a small stiff brush dipped in a yellow and deep green wash and tipped with ultramarine blue. Paint each leaf with a long, thin water-drop stroke that tapers to a fine point, making some of the leaves cross and overlap. To add the two butterflies, follow the instructions on page 16.

Chicks and Trumpet Vine

Step 1

After marking the position of each element of the painting in pencil, begin painting the chicks. Load a soft brush with light black ink and tip it with dark ink. Holding the brush at a 65° angle, paint four fat, egg-shaped water-drop strokes for the head, back, and wings. (For the yellow chick, repeat this process using a lemon yellow wash tipped with burnt sienna.)

Step 2

Dip a very small brush in dark ink, blot the bristles on a paper towel, and hold the brush at a 65° angle to paint the beak and eye. Then use a small stiff brush tipped in dark ink to paint four water-drop strokes along the tip of each wing. The largest stroke should be the farthest from the body. (For the yellow chick, use burnt sienna tipped with medium ink to paint the beak and burnt sienna to paint the tips of the wings.)

Step 3

Saturate a large soft brush with light ink tipped with medium ink and paint one water-drop stroke from the corner of the beak around the bottom of the eye. Apply another water-drop stroke for the chick's chest. (For the yellow chick, use lemon yellow tipped with burnt sienna.) To paint the legs and feet, use a very small brush tipped in dark ink and bone strokes. (For the yellow chick, use burnt sienna tipped in light ink.) Finally add a small stroke of a vermilion wash for the tongue.

Step 4

Now that the chicks are complete,
begin painting the flowers. Use a large
soft brush loaded with vermilion and
tipped with crimson red to paint the
petals with round water-drop strokes,
giving each flower five petals and
leaving the center unpainted. To make
each stroke, flatten the bristles, hold
the brush at a 65° angle, and paint
downward.

Step 5

Without rinsing the soft brush, tip
it with lemon yellow and paint the
cone-shaped bulbs at the base of
each slight- or full-profile flower using
several side-by-side strokes. Then soak
the brush with a vermilion wash and
tip it with lemon yellow to paint the
buds with small water-drop strokes.

Step 6

Next use a large stiff brush dipped in light ultramarine blue and tipped with darker blue to paint the leaves with water-drop strokes. You may want to add multiple strokes to achieve the desired shape.

Step 7

Load a very small brush with a wash of lemon yellow and ultramarine blue. Holding the brush upright, paint branches with bone strokes and connect the flowers to the leaves with short strokes. Add a long vine sweeping down from the main cluster of flowers and curving to the right; you may want to add more blue leaves growing on the vine. Then paint the ladybug as shown in the box at right.

Painting the Ladybug

Saturate a very small brush with cadmium red and tip it with crimson red. Paint two small water-drop strokes for the wings. Rinse out the brush.

Tip the brush with dark ink, and paint one small stroke between the wings for the body. Then add dots for the eyes, antennae, and spots.

Landscape

Step 1

First lightly sketch the scene on paper with a pencil. When there are several elements in a composition—such as a landscape with trees, mountains, sky, and figures—it is important to mark the position of each element before applying ink so you can make proportion adjustments.

Step 2

Next use a small stiff brush dipped in light ink and tipped with dark ink to paint the tree trunk with downward bone strokes. Holding the brush straight up and down, paint the branches with smaller bone strokes. Then add texture to the trunk by filling in the spaces with short bone strokes. Next paint two more trees in the same manner, and add the foliage as shown in the box below. Then, using a very small brush dipped in dark ink, outline the figures in your scene.

Painting the Needles and Leaves

Load a small stiff brush with medium ink and tip it with dark ink. Holding the brush upright, paint the pine needles with downward strokes. Arrange the needles in bundles, allowing some needles to overlap each other.

For the tree on the far right, use a small stiff brush dipped in medium ink and tipped with dark ink. Paint two lines for each downward-turning leaf, holding the brush upright.

Step 3

Paint the outline of the rock as demonstrated in the first step below. Then load a stiff brush with medium ink, tip it with dark ink, and dry the brush slightly on a paper towel to remove some moisture. Apply a series of horizontal strokes to suggest the ground. To give your landscape a sense of space and depth, add the distant mountains and the ground. Reload the stiff brush as described above and trace over the nearest mountain outline; then, holding the brush at a 30° angle, suggest streams of water by sweeping a series of lines from the top of the waterfall to the bottom.

Painting the Rocks

Using a large stiff brush dipped in light ink and tipped with dark ink, paint the outline of the rock. Add shading with a small soft brush dipped in light ink.

Then use a small soft brush dipped in burnt sienna and tipped with light burnt sienna to paint the lower part of the rock around the base, as shown.

To give the rock a cool, stonelike hue, apply a thin wash of indigo blue down the center of the rock. Then add a light blue-green wash to the top surface of the rock.

Step 4

Add the far mountain by retracing the sketch with the stiff brush dipped in medium ink and tipped with dark ink. Now apply a layer of shading to the ground and various planes of the mountains with a light ink wash. To add the colorful hazy mountains in the distance, load a large soft brush with a light burnt sienna wash for the mountain on the right. Hold the brush at a 30° angle and move it from right to left repeatedly to create different shades within the strokes. Paint the blue mountain in the same manner but using a light ultramarine blue wash.

Step 5

Next apply the first layers of color to the other elements in your landscape. Using a soft brush dipped in burnt sienna and tipped with light burnt sienna, stroke the wash on the lower areas of the rock, the mountain, the ground, and the tree trunks. Be sure to leave the waterfall area unpainted. Now use a small stiff brush to add color to the leaves and the needles of the trees with a light blue-green wash (for example, viridian green mixed with cobalt blue). To add color to the waterfall, mix a light blue wash and paint over the water with a soft brush.

Conclusion

Now that you've completed the projects in this book, continue practicing and experimenting with your newfound knowledge of Chinese brush painting. The more you practice, the sooner you'll develop your own unique style and approach. As long as you adhere to the fundamental principles of this timeless art, you can turn any subject into a dynamic Chinese brush painting. Still lifes, landscapes, figures, and animals can all be used to create expressive masterpieces, painted with graceful, deliberate strokes and splashed with vibrant color. We hope you have enjoyed learning about the tools and techniques that make Chinese brush painting such a unique art form, and we wish you the best of luck with your artistic efforts!